Roblox

----- ❧❦❧❦ -----

The Ultimate Game Guide

Table of Contents

Introduction

Congratulations on downloading *Roblox* and thank you for doing so.

The following chapters will discuss things all the way from how to set your Roblox account up all the way on how to create a game and everything in between. When you are done with this book you are going to be able to play Roblox without having too much of an issue.

There are many different parts of Roblox that you are going to need to understand so that your game play is more efficient and you have more fun with the game!

There are plenty of books on this subject on the market, thanks again for choosing this one! Every effort was made to ensure it is full of as much useful information as possible, please enjoy!

Chapter one:

Creating a Roblox Account

Before you can create an account, you need to know that while Roblox is a kid friendly site, admins watch the site to ensure everyone is playing by the rules and keeping it a safe environment.

Step one is to go to the Roblox website which is www.Roblox.com/default.aspx

Step two: select the login button which you will find in the upper left of the screen.

Step three: the website is going to require that you enter some data such as your birthday before you can continue making your account to ensure you are within the age limit.

Note:

There are builder's clubs you can get into that are going to make it to where you can do more. If you get into the club, then make sure that you check the catalog every day so that you can get some of the things that other people are not going to have access to.

You need to remember that there are younger kids who play this so you do not need to be using foul language.

And do not annoy a telamon ever! This can lead to some very bad mistakes.

Chapter two:

Customizing Your Character

With Roblox you can customize your character to fit your image. Anything from shirts to accessories and any other thing that may not do anything, you are going to be able to use. New clothes can be bought with Robux which will be discussed later. Plus, if you do not want to spend money, you can just use the stuff that is free so that you can save up those Robux for something else.

Step one: after you have logged into your account, you are going to go to the menu and select character. The three bars are going to bring up the character customization menu so that you can change how your character appears to others that are playing the game.

Chapter two: Customizing Your Character

Step two: if you want to change your t-shirt, go to the t-shirt table and make any change you want. The shirt is going to appear in a box just to the right of your character so that you can see what it looks like before you choose to equip it.

Step three: individual parts of the body can be customized as well. However, you are only going to be able to wear 1 shirt, 1 pair of pants, 3 hats, 2 arms and legs, 1 face, and 1 package at one time.

Step four: any gear that you want to wear needs to be equip you will see an icon above your character that says wear so that you can put on that outfit.

Chapter three:

Making a New Game

When you are trying to make a new game in Roblox, you are going to open the Roblox studio. If you have already played Roblox, you already having the studio, if you have not, then you are going to need to download the studio.

After the studio, has been opened, there will be a welcome page that is going to point you in the direction that you need to go so that you can open any games that already exist and even create new games. If you so choose, you can browse through the recent articles that have been placed on the Roblox Wiki.

In creating a new game, you are going to select a game template but the basic templates are going to have games that are empty. Theme templates will have games that are built based on specifics that other Roblox users have put into place.

Finally, the gameplay templates are going to have custom game play that has been built in.

Camera controls

The studio has a camera that is going to float freely and will can be moved anywhere that you want it to be moved. When you right click on the camera and move your mouse in the three-dimensional view you can then rotate the camera. The camera can also be zoomed in and out by using a scroll wheel.

Cameras can be moved with keys as well. You can move it forward with the W or S key, side to side with the A and D keys. And finally, up and down with E and Q. Holding down shift is going to make the camera move slower.

Camera focus

The camera can be focused on any object in the game. All you are going to need to do is click on the part or the model and press the F key. This will cause the camera to focus on what you have selected before snapping the camera in closer for a better view. Using rotate will rotate the camera around what you have selected to be the focus of the camera.

Creating new parts

When you click on the parts button you are going to can insert a new part into your game. The arrow is going to be appear that will show you different shapes that you can put into the game to use.

Modifying

Parts can be modified by being clicked on and then dragged to where you want it to be. The part can also be moved and rotated as you see fit. If you want to change the scale, material, or color of the part, you also have this option.

Toolbox

The library or toolbox has a list of decals and models that were created by Roblox their community members. These are going to be free for you to use during your game and when you begin to publish your own, you are going to be able to place them in the toolbox as well.

When you click on an asset, the toolbox is going to automatically place it into your game.

There are different models in the toolbox that are known as high quality models and are going to have a shield icon next to them. These models were checked by the admins of Roblox and are going to work without having to put any work into them.

Play

Your game can be played inside of the studio, but when you are ready to start playing, you are going to hit the play button. From here your character will be inserted into the game.

At the end of your game play, if you should want to edit it again, you will hit the stop button. Any changes that you made will instantly be deleted.

Save

You can quickly save your game onto the servers by going to file and publish. Choose one of the slots to save the game. If you save to a new place, then you are going to need to give your game a name as well as a description. You can also save in a slot that you have already saved in before to overwrite the game that is there.

Roblox does not limit you on how many games you can save.

Chapter four:

Making an Office Building

To build an office building in Roblox, you are going to start with a single window. In continuing, you will use the part button that is going to allow you to put a frame into the game. The last part that you are going to need to add in is the glass that will make the window. Any materials that you use are going to be able to be changed colors.

Here is the part where you are going to make the glass see-through so that you can see what is going on inside of your office building. All you are going to need to do is go to properties and then select the glass portion. From there you will locate the transparency property and set it to somewhere around 0.5.

Chapter four: Making an Office Building

You have only created a single window and you are going to need to have more than that. Instead of going through all the steps that you just went through, you can just copy the one that you already have created and paste it where you are wanting it to go. This is going to be identical to the original one that you created and it is going to save you a lot of time.

The duplicate button can also be used so that you can make copies of the window.

At the point in time that you have made a row of windows, then you can copy it and place another row on top of the first one that you have created. You will keep doing this until you have created your building as tall as you are wanting it to be.

Now you are going to be able to select the entire wall and copy it so that you can make the other walls of your building. All you are going to need to do is rotate the building so that you can place the wall where it needs to be placed.

If you want to save a little bit of time, you can copy two different walls at once and then rotate and fill in the last two walls.

Here you are going to use the scale tool so that you can add in a new part and add the roof of your building.

Chapter five:

Making a Roblox Car

Acar may seem like something complex, but it is extremely simple to build with Roblox. All you are going need to have for your car is a set of wheels, the body of the car, and a seat for your character to sit in.

Going to the parts menu, you will get the main part of the car and from there you are going to use the scale tool so that you can make it longer or taller depending on your preference.

Next comes a cylinder that is going to be one of your wheels. You are going to need to make sure that you use the surface tool to add a hinge onto the wheel or else it is not going to work properly. Be sure that you put the cylinder next to the car body! If you do not, then your car is not going to have wheels and then it is going to be a little hard to get around anywhere.

Chapter five: Making a Roblox Car

Use your duplicate tool to make your other three wheels and rotate the body to make sure that they are in the right place so that all the wheels are actually attached to the body of the car.

The move tool is going to be the tool that you use to get the car off of the ground so that you can set it on the wheels.

The last thing that you need to do is add in a seat. This is where your character is going to sit and with the 3D view, you will insert the object of vehicle seat. The seat should be in the front of the car so that it can be used.

Now that your car works, push play and get in and take it for a spin!

Chapter six:

Moving a Character

When you move a character, you are teleporting them from space to another. This term is going to be in the parts group that includes the movement of things to a different set of coordinates. The property that is used for position will be disconnected from the parts menu or else the model is going to end up breaking. So, you cannot just teleport a character or else you are going to end up breaking them apart.

You are going to need to use the cframe property and cframe data to make sure that you are teleporting a character to the correct place and you are not killing them in the process.

Cframe vs moveto

The moveto function is going to be used in the cframe settings and it will only change the position of the parts in the model. However, the parent property has to be in the workspace as well.

Teleporting all players

You have the ability to teleport all of the players that are in the game by telling each of their characters where to go. You are going to go to the settings in the cframe. But, you need to be careful doing this because you may find that you overlap some of your characters or even accidentally kill them.

Teleporting effects

When you are teleporting your character, you do not have to just teleport them from place to place, you can use a for loop that is going to cause the character to teleport in a different way. Such as, causing individual parts of your body to vanish before you get to where you are wanting to be.

Not only that, you can also rise up out of the ground if you so desire to. All you are going to need to do is make sure that you write the code out for it properly or, go to settings.

Make sure that you are being careful when you are teleporting because you can end up killing your character and having to restart.

Chapter seven:

Teams

Teams are a great way to play with your friends. This is something relatively new that was added to the functionality of the game play in Roblox. Teams can have names and colors all while making it to where you're on a game board to show who is the leader inside of the game.

Enabling the team function

You have to go to the model tab before you can go to the service button. From there you are going to want to go to the advanced section. There you are going to find the teams tab. You will need to select insert so that you can have it enabled in your game play.

Chapter seven: Teams

Adding teams

After you have turned on the ability to have teams, you will then need to add a new team by right clicking on the team tag in your explorer and then inserting the team object.

Names of teams can be changed inside a separate window that will come up listed as properties. Colors can also be changed by changing the team color selections.

Spawning

The location that you spawn in will be objects in Roblox that will play a big part of teams. Once a player has joined in on your game or will come back after they have died is going to be a set location that the team leader has picked. You will know that it is your team's spot because it is going to be the same color as your team color.

Spawn locations can be made by going to the model tab and then selecting the spawn button inside of the game play section. When you select your spawn location, you are going to have a properties window that is open and it will tell you that the spawn color is going to be the same color as the team color. The brick color is going to be different than the team color and this is because the brick color is going to be the color that is displayed but not actually part of the team. Usually the brick color is the same color as the team's color so that there is no confusion among the team players.

Players are allowed to change teams by turning on the setting inside of our properties window for your team. This setting is going to cause a player to automatically join your team if they happen to step on one of the blocks that is one of our spawn points.

Auto assign

The way that Roblox is designed, you are going to automatically be assigned to a team if you join a game that has teams enabled. This game is going to place the player on the team that does not have the same amount of players as the other team.

However, you are able to turn this function off in your team settings so that your team only consist of those who you want to be on it.

Chapter eight:

Create Day or Night Cycles

To be able to do this, you need to have some kind of experience scripting in the game. The code that you run is going to change the appearance of the game.

Time of day

There is no cycle for day or night in Roblox however, you are able to make one yourself if you so desire to. In order to do this, you are going to need to change the time of day by using the setminutesaftermidnight function.

These functions are going to be instructions that the game must follow once it has been printed. The setminutesaftermidnight function is going to be associated with the lighting of the game. In using this function, you are going to need to be specific as to what you are wanting the function to do. This is going to be done much like when you change properties in the game. But, the biggest difference is going to be that the function will be separated by a colon rather than a dot.

The setminutesaftermidnight function is going to be one of the easiest functions that you are able to use in Roblox. All you are going to do is place the numbers between the set of parentheses in the code so that it shows exactly how many minutes after midnight you are wanting your world be be at. So, if you want it to be 2 am you are going to put a 2 in the code.

Changing the time of day can be done whenever you want it to be changed.

If you change the game time several times right in a row, you are going to end up landing on the last time that you selected. The game will have gone through all the other times that you wanted it to go through, but it is going to go faster than you are going to be able to register.

So, to change this so that we can see the time actually changing you will enter in the function known as wait.

The wait function is going to pause the game changing time for however many seconds we are wanting it to wait. So, we can have it wait for one second or longer if you want it all depends on you.

Looping

Changing the time is only going to work for a short time period. But, if you are wanting to get the day to change after an x amount of minutes or even hours, thousands of lines of code will need to be written. But, thanks to Roblox, there is a way to get around this and it is known as looping.

Loops are going to be a series of code that will constantly repeat itself until a condition has been met to cause the loop to terminate. If you want the loop to never be terminated, you will use a while loop.

Street lamps

Street lamps are going to automatically turn on and off depending on the time of day. But, you are going to need to put one in your game before this can work.

First you will use the light part so that a neon material is created so that it will glow. The next part that is going to be added is the point light and this will allow for the light to reflect off all the parts that are around the light.

Chapter eight: Create Day or Night Cycles

Colors can be changed on the street lamp as well as the brightness and how far it will shine.

Chapter nine:

Mouse Appearance

You can change the appearance of your mouse so that it reflects who you are and is not just the default mouse that everyone has.

Mouse icon

To change the appearance of your mouse, you are going to go to the local script and change the script to add in decals so that your mouse appears how you want it to be.

Hiding the mouse

Seeing the mouse is entirely optional, you can turn this on or off by using the mouse icon property in your settings in the local script.

Chapter nine: Mouse Appearance

Locking the mouse

If you do not want your mouse to move, you can lock it with the mouse behavior setting. This property will make it to where the mouse is locked in the center of the screen and you will have to use the same code that you use to lock it to unlock it by setting it back to its default settings.

Chapter ten:

Game Passes

Agame pass is a feature that allows the creator to gain special abilities or perks for their game. This has to be bought in the game.

Creating a game pass

A game pass is free to someone who plays Roblox. You do not have to be in the builders club to gain a game pass. But, you are going to have to go about getting a game pass one of two ways. You can either go to your profile and select the button that says "create a game pass." But, you are going to need to make sure that it is placed under an active place. If it is not, then you will need to go to the develop page and select configure from a menu that drops down so that you can choose a place to create a game pass.

After you have done this, you will follow the instructions on the page to create the game pass.

Chapter ten: Game Passes

Selling your pass

Once you have gotten your pass created, your pass will not show up on your page. To get it to show, you have to put it up for sale or make it free. This can be done by going to the page that the pass is on and selecting the options at the top right. From here you will configure your pass so that it can be sold.

Be sure that you save your changes before you exit the page!

Buying a game pass

Game passes can also be bought, but they have to be bought from where the creator has placed it. You need to go to that page first and then go to where you see the section that is labeled game pass. From there, you are going to be able to see a name and description of all the passes that are available as well as a button that says "buy now" if the pass is able to be sold.

There are some developers that use the marketplace to do transactions in the game for other players. This is going to be done by using a method known as prompt purchase so that the buyer is prompted to buy the item that they are looking at.

Do not expect this to be done by everyone though because it is not. It just depends on the developer.

Other

- The first game pass that was put into Roblox was known as a game pass testing

- The game passes were not put into the game until September of 2012.

- The very first game was called "You are worthy" and had the location attached to it.

- A game pass will use the texture known as badge.

Chapter eleven:

Robux

Robux is kind of like any other game, it is the currency that can be used in game to buy stuff. There are three different methods that you can use to gain robux so that you do not run low and are still able to get the stuff that you want that costs these green dollars.

Method one:

Step one: join the builders club. Each day that passes, members of the builder's club are able to gain robux just for their membership. However, it is going to depend on which level of the club that you occupy that will depend on how much you get each day.

To join the builder's club, it is going to take real world money, and there are a few things that you need to remember.

Chapter eleven: Robux

- Tix has been removed so players who use NBC are finding it harder to get robux.

- When you first purchase builder's club, you are going to get an extra hundred robux.

- ONC members get sixty a day and it costs sixty-five dollars a month.

- A regular builders club member is only going to get fifteen robux a day for the price of fifteen dollars a month

- TBC members get thirty-five a day for the price of twenty-five a month.

Method two:

Step one: buy and sell

There are collectible items that you are going to be able to buy or sell. When you are going to buy these items, you are going to need to have a lot of robux already in your account.

In order to sell them, you need to be a member of the builder's club and be able to find someone to who is going to pay the price that you are wanting for that item.

It is wise to set your prices reasonable so that you are able to find buyers.

Step two: trade

There are going to be other members in the Roblox universe that are looking for what you have! Thanks to the builder's club, you are able to add robux to trades so if you have something that you are wanting to trade and someone else has something that is of more value, you can get robux and the item.

Step three: sell your wardrobe

With the builders club, you have the ability to create custom shirts and pants for your character, but, instead of just letting the ones that you no longer use "collect dust" why not sell them for a little bit of extra gaming cash.

Step four: create and design

If you are good at scripting or creating designs, you can sell them. Scripting is a very valuable skill when it comes to Roblox and you can actually sell yourself so that you can do some scripting for someone and get robux for the job that you do for them.

Chapter eleven: Robux

Should you want to do this, it is better that you start out with a low number of orders so that your designs can be shown off and then others will come to you. Also, make sure that you do not take on more than you can handle or else you may end up with some very angry customers.

Method three:

Step one: create a game pass.

Game passes will give you access to bonuses no matter what game you find yourself playing. Even if you are not in a builder's club you can create them therefore selling them for robux. If you are not in a builder's club you are only going to get ten percent of what you sell it for, but that is better than not getting anything at all!

Step two: add gear

The add gear setting can be turned off or on in your settings. This buttons allows other people to place gear in other people's space. If you turn it on, then anyone who purchases gear in your page is going to receive the gear in the game.

Step three: VIP

A vip server is a server where people have to pay to get onto it. If you create one, then you can charge up to a hundred robux for them to play on your server.

Chapter twelve:

Teleporting Between Two Places

Teleporting can not only get you from one place to the next without having to use the website, it can also get you from one game to another. You will find this service listed under the asset service selection

Use

You can call upon the teleporting services with a script or local script. This function is going to allow the script to turn the player into an object so that it can be moved.

Like many of the functions that you will use when you are using teleporting, you are going to need to have an id in place for where you are wanting to move your character.

Chapter twelve: Teleporting Between Two Places

If your destination is in the same game, then you can teleport from your current place to the id of the place that you are wanting to go. In order to get the id, you are going to go to the game explorer and right click. From here you can copy the id to the clipboard so that you are sure that you are not missing a number.

If all else fails, you can get the id from the Roblox website.

Valid destinations

There are some limitations to where you are able to teleport. You are only able to teleport inside of the same game or to the starting place of a new game.

Chapter thirteen:

Pathfinding

As you go about moving a character, you are going to discover that it is not as simple as it sounds. There are often times going to be obstacles in your path that you are going to need to find a way around. If you just try and keep going, you are most likely going to end up getting your character stuck. Other times, you are going to notice that your character needs to be moved to a specific point. That is where the pathfinding service is going to come in handy because it is going to create a nice clean path for you to be able to follow.

Path

When you are using the pathfinding service, you are going to use the path object. This will be a series of points that will have a starting point as well as an ending point to ensure that the path is completely clear. If there is not a clear path, then a new path will be made.

Chapter thirteen: Pathfinding

Creating the path

The computer is going to make the path that your character is going to follow using the computerawpathasync function. There are three things that the computer is going to need in order to get the path. First it is going to need the end of the path, next it will need the start of the path, and the last thing it needs is the maximum distance that the path is going to be allowed to be.

Evaluating

The path finding services is going to evaluate the path to make sure that there is not going to be anything in the way. This status will be put under the status of the path so that you can view it and determine if the path can be used or not.

Failfinishnotempty: the path failed to compute because an ending point was not entered.

Success: the path was found successfully and can be used.

Failstartnotempty: there is not start point therefore the path was not computed.

Closestnopath:the path is not real and you need to go to the closest one

Closestoutofrange: the max distance is out of range and the path is going to be returned to the closest point that can be achieved inside of the maximum distance that is set.

The path will be what determines if you are able to use the path or if you have to reconfigure it with a set of new parameters. You may even need to choose a different behavior for your character to follow.

Using the path

The path is going to be nothing more than a table of points that is read by the get points coordinates method. The table will store all the points from start to finish in order for the path to be followed.

You should remember that this service is not going to make your character move, all it will do is show you the path that he or she is allowed to follow. In order to move along the path you will need to use your move functions.

Rechecking

Since playing Roblox is going to be dynamic, there could end up being things that land in the path that you are using even after you have created it. The path will then need to be recalculated so that the object can either be removed or the path can be modified.

You need to know that if you recalculate your path, it will be very expensive and therefore you should only do it if you absolutely have to.

To check the path, you can use the checkocclusionasync function. In using this function, you are going to be checking to see if there are any points in the path that have become obstructed. If it turns out that there is an obstruction, then the index for the path will be listed as to where it has been obstructed.

In recalculating the path, you are going to be able to get around the obstruction without getting too far off your path.

Emptycutoff

There are some other problems that you may run into such as thin floors. Many thin floors that you find are going to be empty being that there is not enough space to put anything down. This is done because of how the floor is calculated into the game.

The service that finds your paths is going to divide the world into 4x4x4 cubes that are going to be known as voxels. From there these voxels are going to be checked to see just how empty they are so that the path can be determined.

A voxel will be considered empty if it is less than sixteen percent full.

There are two solutions that you can use when you run into a thin floor. First you, you can try and make the floor thicker so that more room is taken up by the voxels. Or you can use the empty cutoff in order to lower the value of the voxels.

Using the emptycutoff is going to have its advantages because it will preserve the look of the level, but the paths on your level are going to be changed.

Chapter fourteen:

Customizing Your Loading Screen

When games get bigger, there are more assets that have to be used and thus loading time is going to be longer. Instead of having a level appear as incomplete, there are going to be preferences as to what kind of loading screen is seen while these details are loaded into the game. Of course, the game is going to give you a loading screen, but you can always create your own.

Disabling the default

First, you need to turn the default loading screen off. You will go into the local script and use the replicated first service that will replicate the instances to your client before the game actually loads. When you use the local script you will be making sure that the script of your choosing is going to run before any script by the client. You

are also going to be removing the default loading
screen so that the Roblox loading screen is no
longer used.

Creating a screen

The loading screen is going to use GUI elements
that are provided by Roblox. Some of these
elements are going to be found in the player's gui
which is inside of the local script.

GUI elements are going to be stored with either
the replicated first method or they will be created
inside of the script so that they are instantly
moved over to the player's gui. There is a top bar
that is going to be made to look opaque so that
any geometry can be hid behind it.

You need to take note that there may end up
being a small delay as you wait for the player gui.
The default loading screen behind hid will make
you wait before the gui is loaded and the game is
then made visible but only for a second. You
should try and wait for the player gui to load
before you try and start with the initial screen
that you are wanting to see before you go about
hiding the loading gui that is there by default.

Hiding the loading screen

There are going to be times that the loading screen does not need to be seen because all of the details behind it have already loaded. It does not matter if you have set your loading screen to play longer than the time that is needed to load or not, you can still get rid of it whenever the game is ready to be played.

You can use the request queue size or isloaded functions to see the content that is inside of the game. However, you are not going to see the status of the load so you should try and set your screen to only be up for as long as it takes for your game to normally load.

Custom loading screens with teleporting service

When characters are being teleported, a custom loading screen can be use, but you will need to set different parameters for it so that the screen only plays as long as it takes for your character to be loaded into his new spot.

Chapter fifteen:

Musical Buttons

There is a button that can be added to the game that will either enable or disable your background music at will.

Adding buttons

The button is going to be added like a two dimensional element would be added. You will first insert the screen gui into the starter gui. From there, the image button will be used to insert the audio image. The position can be changed depending on where you are wanting it on your screen.

There has to be two different images used for your buttons. One for when the music is on and one for when the music is off. Most commonly you will see a speaker for when it is on, and a speaker with a line through it when the music is off.

Chapter fifteen: Musical Buttons

When you are looking at the view tab of your game, you will go to the game explorer. From here you will right click on the asset button and then go to add multiple images. This is going to be where you can add the two images that tell you about the music.

In clicking on the image property, a new window will pop up and you will need to add the image to the proper selection. You are also able to make the button smaller if you want so that you are not seeing a huge button when you are playing. To do this, you will use the size property.

Adding music

It is at this point in time that you are going to be able to add in music. Files for music will either need to be mp3 or ogg files. When adding the audio file, you are going to need to go to the develop page and then the audio tab for Roblox. This is where the file will be uploaded and then given its appropriate name.

Files that are uploaded need to be at least a hundred and twenty seconds long or even shorter and if possible kept to eight thousand one hundred and ninety-two kilobytes. It is going to cost around a hundred robux to upload an audio file.

Sound does not need to be uploaded right away if that is how you want to deal with it.

After you have uploaded your audio clip, it will be available on your list of sounds on your developer page. You will simply click on the name and then go to the page that it is assigned to. From here you are going to look at the URL and make sure to get the id number which will fall at the end of the URL.

Here is where you are ready to load the file into the game. Right click on your image button and insert the new noise. It is inside of the soundid box that you are going to put down that number that you copied so that the proper sound is added to the game. The loop property should also be enabled so that the sound keeps going.

Binding function to button clicks

Before you can say that you are finished, you will need to do a bind function that is going to allow the mouse to control when the music is on or when it is off. The local script is going to be used for this.

The local script will be similar to the scripted objected but it is going to only control what is going on locally to your machine only. Regular scripts will manipulate things that are on the server.

So, the determination of if the music plays or not will be a local script rather than a regular script.

You will insert the script into the image that you have put on the screen. The button will first need to be made into a variable so that the sound that is inserted is going to play properly. Being that sounds will sometimes take a minute or two to load, the function waitforchild is going to be used.

The function is going to need to be defined by a button click. Therefore, when a button is clicked, the music will stop or it is going to start playing. This function will be defined by the mouse button click event so that the program does what you are telling it to do.

Chapter sixteen:

MatchMaking

When it comes to playing in a competitive game, you are going to want to be with players who have the same skill set as you. Roblox actually can split players into teams without taking into account what they are able to do. But, you can bypass this by using the elo rating system and get matched with someone who is going to be equal to you.

There are going to be many different features that are used in matchmaking and there are several individual components that you will need to pay attention to or else it is not going to work the way that it is supposed to.

Elo rating

This system is a system that is used in the ranking of players. There are many games that use this very same system when they are working on matching players together. It allows the players to see how they are doing compared to the other players that are in that game. Not only that, but it makes matchmaking simpler so that the players are matched on an equal level. In addition to making the match it can also predict who is going to win.

The elo system is based off wins and losses. Whenever two players have finished a game, then their rankings are adjusted based on how the game turned out. In the event that a high ranked player beats a player that is low ranked, then the higher ranking player is going to get a small increase in his ranking, but if it is the other way around, the lower player will get a larger increase.

Matchmaking lobbies

There is going to be a lobby that is going to be where the players are matched together. When a match has been made, the players will then be moved to the place where they are playing the game against each other.

Player rank

After a player, has entered the game, they are given a rank. That number can be any number that the system has open. Therefore, the player is going to be able to move up or down in the rankings without going into the negative numbers. If the player has played before, then their rank will come from the database.

Rank list

After players, have been matched, it is going to be best that a structure be in place so that the players can be searchable with rank. There are multiple structures that are going to work for this.

Chapter seventeen:

Get Out There and Advertise

You are able to create ads on Roblox for whatever it is that you are wanting to sell. The ads will be images that the user uploads so that when the image is clicked, the clicker is taken to the thing that is being sold.

Advertising

Your ad is created by other users depending on where it is going to be displayed. The advertiser is going to bid by using robux that are in their account. At the point in time that a page loads, the code will decide which ads they should see. So, not every user is going to see your ad.

Auction

An advertiser is not going to buy the space that is used on Roblox. Instead, they are going to bid on it in an auction because there is only going to be a limited amount of space that is available for advertising. When a player pays more, they are going to gain more impressions.

Essentially, spending twice as much is going to get you twice as many impressions as someone who does not spend that much.

With Roblox, there are three different kinds of advertising that you can use. A banner, a large rectangle ad, or a skyscraper. The banner ad is not going to be able to go into any other slot and same with the other ads.

There are only going to be specific pages that ads are going to be able to be shown on depending on what is purchased. A banner can be put on any ad, but a large rectangle is only going to be shown on user pages.

Definitions

Impression: one impression is given for every user that sees the ad.

Clicks: one click will be given for every user that clicks on your ad.

CTR: the click through rate is going to be clicks and impressions together. If someone sees your ad and clicks on it, then your CTR will be at one hundred percent. The better the ad, the higher the CTR.

Run: when the display of an ad is bidded on and then launched to be run. This is only going to last around twenty-four hours.

Banner: an ad that is only 728 x 90.

Skyscraper: an ad that is 160 x 600

Large rectangle: an ad that is 300 x 250

Skyscraper: an ad that is 160 x 600

Large rectangle: an ad that is 300 x 250

Campaign: the ad campaign is going to be ads that come in a series that are going to be for the same product. But, the ad system on Roblox is not going to support campaigns.

CPC: Cost per click. This is not going to show up on your CPC but it can be helpful. Bad ads are going to have a larger CPC than other ads.

Creating ads

When you want to create an ad, you are going to go to the page that you want it placed on and select the link that is labeled as advertise this place that appears below your picture.

Once you have clicked on it, you are going to get a new page that walks you through the steps of creating an ad.

Using an ad

After an ad has been created, it can now be displayed wherever you want it to be displayed. You will need to go to your profile and then go to the ad inventory. It is here that you are going to find your ads so that they can be on the site.

All you are going to need to do is select run ad and from there you are going to bid money so that your ad can be placed over someone else's.

Chapter eighteen:

CreatePlace vs SavePlace

There is an API that will allow the user to create and even save places through their script. When you look at the introduction of the data and its features, the builder is going to be able to make games that are going to create places that are going to belong to the builder. This will then open up more possibilities such as MMORPG games.

Usage

The asset service function is going to copy any places that exist in the game and save it to the player's inventory. There is going to be a new place that will part of the original game and it is going to have access to all the same stores of data that the other game did.

Enabling creating and saving

You have something that you have to do before you are able to use a template with the create place or even before you can save it with save place. This is to enable them for your place. You will log into Roblox and go to the develop tab. From there you are going to go to places on the menu that is on the left side of your screen.

From here you are going to see a list of all the places that are inside of your inventory. Hitting the configure button, you are going to use the template that you have selected on the game of your choosing. This is going to enable you to set the place as being able to be used as a template as well as being saved.

Adding template places

You will add a place template by logging into Roblox and going to the developer tab. When you select games you can choose the configure button and then go to places so that the place can be added. All of your other places can be added to the game as long as they are able to be used as template for the create place function.

Make sure that you have enabled the create place or else you cannot use this function.

Limits

The save place as well as the create place are going to be mechanics that are throttled. When you are using these functions, you have to be sure that you have something that will capture your exceptions and do what it is supposed to do.

Key API

Chapter nineteen:

Saving All Your Data for Later

The information that is stored on the servers can be saved by the user. This is going to store all the data that is needed between sessions for users. Therefore, the user is still going to be able to progress through the game even though they leave and come back.

Setting up data

Before you can save your data, you need to set the system up so that your movements are tracked. This can be done by using the module script in your game. This script is going to be referenced from various other scripts. It also has the ability to be set up to have a table returned to the user. In this case, the scripts that are referenced are going to use module script to access values that are listed inside of that table.

These values can be other functions or other tables.

Saving data

After the system has been set up to track data, you can now store it to the database that is used by Roblox by using the function data stores. You will need to add in a variable to the script with the data store function. With this function there are going to be parameters that will be the name of the store where all the data is. Should there not be any data store, then Roblox is going to create one for you.

Your data stores can be named whatever you want it to be named. Just keep in mind that your data store is going to be shared between all of the places that are in your game. If there are multiple places in your game, you will have access to the same data store so you should name them all the same name.

With the variable that is holding the data store, you are going to change how the player data function works. The data store is going to be able to hold any information that the player has used in the game. If the function is not returned, then nothing has been saved for that player therefore new data is going to be saved.

You need to make sure that your data can handle any events like when your game crashes. This is not going to happen often, but you do not want to lose any of the progress that you have made. While you may think that you should save each time you make a change to your game, the data store is going to limit how many times it can be accessed.

When the data store is accessed too much, then it is going to slow down how fast it is able to access the data. So, there is a timer that is going to make it to where there is a certain amount of time that has to pass before the data store is accessed once again.

As a game automatically saves, it is going to save each cycle that the data store is going to be able to be accessed. With some games, the data store can be accessed sooner than others.

Handling failures with data store

The data stores on Roblox are very reliable, but if you are saving your data, you may need to prepare for the worst just in case it happens. If you cannot connect to the data store, then our game needs to be able to handle this as well as tell you that it cannot save your game progress.

One of the best ways for this to be handled is to make sure that the data store access is retried a few times to make sure that it is truly not connecting. If it fails every time, then you are going to need to let the player know that it cannot save any data. It is going to depend on how dependent your game is on the data store on how you are to going proceed. You will either keep going with your game without saving, or you will stop and just wait for the data store to be able to be accessed again.

If the data store cannot communicate with any script, then you are going to get an error that is going to terminate the program and all of the script that is inside of it. The script needs to be prepared by having a backup. The pcall function is going to hopefully catch the error before the the program can crash.

The function is going to be retried multiple times before it can be said that it is going to fail or succeed. This is also where the function is going to be defined by the parameters that you are going to put into place to determine how many times it is retried.

If the starting of the data then there are going to be several other things that you are going to be able to do so that you can safeguard your data.

There is one approach that is going not going to allow any saving to go on with the game data. This allows the game to not overwrite any of the old data.

Chapter twenty:

Go to School at the Roblox University

The Roblox university is also known as Roblox and there are different lessons that will help you get through Roblox. Every lesson is going to take you from the very beginning and work all the way up so that you are able to know what tools are offered by Roblox. All the lessons will start at easy to those that are not so easy depending on how far in the game you are.

Roblox racing

You can learn how to make a racing game with Roblox all by using the studio tools. The tools in the studio are going to allow you to build your car, your tracks, and even how to work with the scripting system that is inside of Roblox.

Chapter twenty-one:

Managing the Game Memory

When you are managing the memory, you are going to be managing the computer's memory on the system level. This is going to be an important part of the memory management that is going to allow for things to move dynamically so that the program can do what it needs to do whenever it is requested, it is also going to be free to be reused even after it is no longer needed.

Basics

There are some local variables that will recycle automatically even after there are no references to them. This is just another feature that you will find in Lua that is going to be referred to as garbage collection.

Chapter twenty-one: Managing the Game Memory

As a memory dumps an object, that means that there is not going to be referenced any longer in the program, thus the memory is going to maintain the object's existence until it has been released so that some new data can take the previous objects place.

Roblox works in a similar fashion. However, there are three things that are going to stop you from being able to collect the garbage.

- Another object

- The object is a descendant

- A variable

Chapter twenty-two:

Fighting Lag

S ometimes when you are working with network games, there is the problem of lag that is unavoidable. If your game is using the filtering function, then you are going to have a number different functions that are going to be able to be used that are going end up lagging your game. However, you can use a few functions that are going to help you to get used to this lag and use it to your advantage.

Lagging- the source

Why does lag happen? When you tell a game to do something, it is going to read the command that you have told it to do, however, the communication from server to server is going to take longer than what it normally does. It is going to be because the signal that is being used for your computer is going to have to pass through different airwaves before it is actually able to carry out your command.

Chapter twenty-two: Fighting Lag

Cannon lag

In the Roblox game, laggy cannons, you are going to have four different cannons that you are going to have to aim towards targets that are moving. Each time that the target is affected, then there is going to be some lag time that is exaggerated however, every cannon target is going to address this lag with a different method.

Some of the methods are going to handle the lag better than other targets.

Blue cannon

In the game, the blue cannon is not going to try and fight any of the lag. Hitting the fire key is going to make the cannon fire noise, but you will not see it fire for a few seconds after the noise has been made.

When you look at the script for the blue cannon, there is going to be a variable that is known as active cannon. This variable is going to work for the blue cannon. There will be no effect on how the blue cannon handles the lag even if you mess with the code.

Watch your code

The function known as bad cannon strategy is going to look like it will be fine and work perfectly. But, when the cannon fires, there is going to be a big explosion. The problem is going to be that the lag is going to be ignored completely which is good, but if you want to have a good game, you are going to need to have a little lag there.

Orange cannon

The orange cannon is going to be just like the blue cannon, however, it is going to modify the strategies that it uses to try and fight the lag. The only real change that you are going to see in the orange cannon's code is going to be the first line. When the orange cannon uses the remote function it is called the fire cannon function. The remote event is going to be a signal that is going to come from the client and go to the server while the remote function is going to from the client to server and then return.

Since the client is expecting something to be returned, it is going to wait for that value to be returned so that it can be moved to the local script. The orange cannon takes advantage of this and fire better so that the cannonball is sent before the explosion.

Synchronize the experience

While the blue cannon might not make sense in the real world the game is still going to be fun because it is not going to break the player's imagination. But, looking at the orange cannon is going to synchronize the events that occur between the client and the server.

Red cannon

The orange cannon may solve the unsynchronized problem, but it is still going to be touched by lag. When you press the fire key, there is going to be a delay before you see the game do anything at all. This is known as input lag. The cannonball cannot be fired no matter what you try and do to the code.

The player can give some feedback to the developers though so that they know about how the game is responding. When the fire button is pressed on the red cannon, then the cannon fuse is going to burn before it fires the cannon. You will however keep hearing the fuse burn even after it has exploded.

While there is still a delay between pressing the fire button and the cannon actually firing, the red cannon is going to feel more natural to the player because they are not going to notice the lag that they are experiencing.

Input lag

There is nothing worse than input lag because you are going to feel as if you are disconnected from the game. It is going to be necessary to have a response between the player's input and the game so that they know that the request has been heard.

Purple target

The purple cannon and the red cannon work exactly the same. The only difference is how the purple target is going to react because all the targets are going to work differently.

If an orange, red, or blue target is hit, then there will be a delay. But, if you hit the purple target, you are not going to see the delay because there is not going to be any lag.

From what you have learned with the filtering enabled function, the score from the player is going to be put into the database on the server.

Chapter twenty-two: Fighting Lag

This is going to cause a delay when the score is updated.

While the server is the one that is responsible for telling you if the target was hit or not, the user is going to be able to see if they hit the target or not. The worst thing that can happen is that you are going to disagree with the way that the computer judged it and therefore your score is not going to be updated.

Testing

Lag can be simulated in the Roblox studio by going to the settings and then to the incoming replication lag that is inside of the network option. The number have to be adjusted so that you can see how bad the lag truly can be.

Chapter twenty-three:

Making a Painting

In making a painting you are going to need to start out with a frame. The frame should be thin and you can change the parts in the form factor property under custom.

After you have published your game on Roblox, you will find that it is easier for you to add images to a game that is published rather than one that has not been published.

Decals are going to added to make an image for our painting. You need to right click on the back paneling of the picture frame and then insert an object. Here is where you are going to choose a decal.

In the properties window, you are going to need to locate a decal, ensure that you have selected it before the properties window is opened. After it has been opened, right click on texture and then hit add image.

Chapter twenty-three: Making a Painting

Yet another window will be opened so that you can pick the image off your computer. After you have gotten the file that you want, you will hit the create button and it will appear in the game.

All kinds of images can be used as decals, and they do not have to just be paintings!

Chapter twenty-four:

Tips and Tricks for Roblox

- A skateboard can be inserted into the game by using the plane tool. The plane tool can also be used to fly your skateboard around like a normal plane.

- Mini tanks can be inserted and should you drive it off the base, then you will have a floating mini tank.

- If you want to chat with someone you are going to hit the backslash button and then type in what it is that you are wanting to say before hitting the enter button. Make sure your game is full screen so you can see the chat bar that is at the bottom of the screen.

- Press CTRL and F1 at the same time to freeze your game.

Chapter twenty-four: Tips and Tricks for Roblox

- Using blogs instead of making websites actually makes it easier when you are an ambassador

- If you hold the up key when you are playing your character and then hit s, you can cause your character to do the moonwalk.

- Games limit you to 45 minutes of play.

- If you use a head roll and ninja make, you can make hair.

- Always stay updated on Roblox news.

- If you want to see how much Robux you are going to get use tradecurrency to see the exchange rate.

- Rest on a set of stairs so that a body part is touching them. Teleport so that you can get extra points. For every body part that is teleported, the more points you will get.

Conclusion

Thank for making it through to the end of *Roblox*, let's hope it was informative and able to provide you with all of the tools you need to achieve your goals whatever it may be.

The next step is to download Roblox and start creating your world! If you are not ready to make your own world, you can play on words that are already created until you get the hang of it.

You are going to experience new things with Roblox even if you have been playing video games for most of your life. Do not expect that this is going to be an easy game, because while it may see easy, there are a lot of intricate moving parts that make up this game.

Finally, if you found this book useful in anyway, a review on Amazon is always appreciated!

Thank you and good luck!